CUTTING-EDGE TECHNOLOGY

ALL ABOUT
LAB-GROWN MEAT

by Rachel Kehoe

T0014971

FOCUS
READERS.

NAVIGATOR

WWW.FOCUSREADERS.COM

Focus Readers is distributed by North Star Editions: sales@northstareditions.com | 888-417-0195

Produced for Focus Readers by Red Line Editorial.

Content Consultant: Reza Ovissipour, PhD, Assistant Professor, Department of Food Science and Technology, Virginia Polytechnic Institute and State University

Photographs ©: David Parry/EMPPL PA Wire/AP Images, cover, 1, 4–5; Shutterstock Images, 7, 8–9, 10, 14, 19, 20–21, 24–25, 27, 28; Terry Chea/AP Images, 12–13, 17; Aleph Farms/ Cover Images/AP Images, 22

Library of Congress Cataloging-in-Publication Data
Names: Kehoe, Rachel, author.
Title: All about lab-grown meat / by Rachel Kehoe.
Description: Lake Elmo, MN : Focus Readers, [2023] | Series: Cutting-edge
  technology | Includes index. | Audience: Grades 4-6
Identifiers: LCCN 2022031704 (print) | LCCN 2022031705 (ebook) | ISBN
  9781637394724 (hardcover) | ISBN 9781637395097 (paperback) | ISBN
  9781637395790 (ebook pdf) | ISBN 9781637395462 (hosted ebook)
Subjects: LCSH: Cultured meat--Juvenile literature. | Meat--Moral and
  ethical aspects--Juvenile literature.
Classification: LCC TP447.M4 K44 2023 (print) | LCC TP447.M4 (ebook) |
  DDC 664/.9--dc23/eng/20220820
LC record available at https://lccn.loc.gov/2022031704
LC ebook record available at https://lccn.loc.gov/2022031705

Printed in the United States of America
Mankato, MN
012023

ABOUT THE AUTHOR

Rachel Kehoe is a science writer and children's author. She has published several books and articles on science, technology, and climate change.

TABLE OF CONTENTS

CHAPTER 1

WHAT'S FOR LUNCH?

You sit down at a restaurant. A waiter puts two burger patties on the table. One of them is a regular burger. The other was grown in a lab. You try to tell the difference.

You inspect both burgers. Then you sniff them. One of the burgers looks

The first lab-grown burger was made by scientists at Maastricht University.

lighter than the other. Otherwise, both look and smell the same.

You cut a small slice of the first burger and eat it. Then you taste the other burger. Both have the same texture. They are equally chewy. They also have a similar flavor. You can't tell which burger came from the lab.

Meat is an animal product. This means it comes from the body of an animal. Meat is mostly animal muscle. So, animals die to produce this food. Methods for raising and killing these animals can be cruel. They can also harm the environment.

Lab-grown meat offers a solution. This type of meat still comes from animals.

To meet the demand for meat, farms and ranches raise huge numbers of animals.

But instead of killing the animals, scientists take just a small group of cells from their bodies. The animals can keep living. Meanwhile, scientists use the cells to grow **tissue** in a lab or factory. For this reason, lab-grown meat is sometimes called "cultured meat." It is also called "cell-based meat."

CHAPTER 2

PROBLEMATIC PROTEIN

Meat provides an important source of **protein** for people around the world. In 2021, more than 70 billion animals were raised for food. They included chickens, cows, sheep, and pigs.

All these animals take up huge amounts of land and resources. In many places, forests are cleared to make space

In 2020, people raised nearly 94 million cattle in the United States alone.

Animals need lots of food. Chemicals used to grow this food can get into nearby land and water.

for farms and ranches. These changes destroy the habitats of wild plants and animals.

In 2018, more than 75 percent of Earth's farmland was used to feed livestock. These animals need lots of water. So do the plants they eat. Plus, the animals and plants are often treated with chemicals that can harm the environment.

In addition, some animals release methane when they digest food. Methane is a **greenhouse gas**. As more of it enters Earth's atmosphere, **climate change** gets even worse. To address these problems, scientists encourage people to eat less meat.

ANIMAL WELFARE

Many livestock animals are raised on factory farms. These huge farms hold tens of thousands of animals. Cows, pigs, and chickens are often kept in small, dirty pens. They have little space to move. Not all farms treat animals badly. In fact, some try using **ethical**, Earth-friendly ways to produce meat. But these efforts won't be enough to fight climate change.

CHAPTER 3

MAKING MEAT IN A LAB

Lab-grown meat starts with **stem cells**. Most cells in the body have set functions. Stem cells are different. They can change to make other types of cells. They also multiply quickly.

To grow lab meat, scientists remove a small number of stem cells from an animal. They use this sample to develop

At labs, workers prepare mixtures of nutrients to help cells grow and multiply.

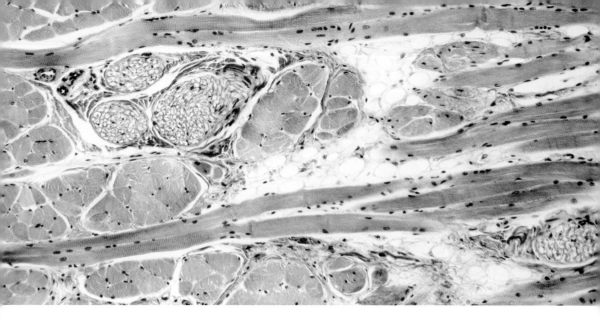

 Tissue forms when cells join together. The cells in muscle tissue form long fibers.

cell lines. These cells grow to become fat and muscle cells. The muscle cells are separated and placed inside a tank. This tank is called a bioreactor. Inside it, the cells continue to divide and grow. A dropper feeds them nutrients. The cells are also given growth factor solution. **Hormones** in this solution help the cells develop.

The cells naturally join together. Then they are placed in a ring of gel. The cells attach to this surface. After a few weeks, they form long strands of tissue. At this point, the meat looks similar to ground beef. So, scientists must shape

THE FIRST BURGER

In 2013, the first lab-grown burger was cooked and eaten. Scientists took stem cells from a cow's shoulder. The cells grew to make more than 20,000 strips of muscle. The strips combined to make a beef patty. Three people tried a bite. All enjoyed the texture. But they agreed it tasted bland. Their feedback gave scientists ideas for how to improve lab-grown meat.

it. They often make burgers, nuggets, or sausages.

Other meat shapes, such as chicken wings, are more complicated. These cuts of meat have fat and bones. Their texture is different, too. For example, chicken has a springy texture. To mimic it, scientists make a gelatin mixture. They spin it until it makes tiny fibers. Then, they add stem cells. As the stem cells grow, they mix them with the strings. This gives the lab-grown meat more structure. It becomes chewy, like regular chicken.

Because lab-grown meat is just muscle, it creates much less waste than raising livestock. Some parts of animals' bodies

This chicken was grown at a lab in California.

can't be eaten. These parts are often thrown away. Living animals also create manure. Lab-grown meat avoids these problems. One cell sample can make 22,000 pounds (10,000 kg) of meat.

BIOREACTOR

After stem cells are taken from an animal's body, they need a place to grow. That's what a bioreactor is for. A bioreactor is a machine that holds living cells. It provides everything the cells need.

Many bioreactors have tanks shaped like cylinders. They are made of metal or glass. Inside the tanks are fats, minerals, and proteins. Cells need all these substances to grow. Large tubes bring these substances into the tank.

Animal cells also need oxygen. Inside a body, cells receive oxygen from blood. But a bioreactor doesn't have blood. Instead, it passes air through a pipe. This delivers oxygen to the cells as tiny bubbles.

Finally, a bioreactor must keep cells warm. A thermometer measures the temperature inside the

BIOREACTOR PARTS

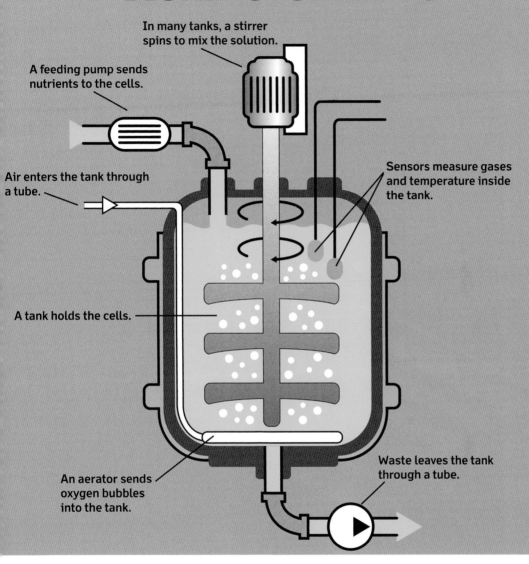

In many tanks, a stirrer spins to mix the solution.

A feeding pump sends nutrients to the cells.

Air enters the tank through a tube.

Sensors measure gases and temperature inside the tank.

A tank holds the cells.

An aerator sends oxygen bubbles into the tank.

Waste leaves the tank through a tube.

tank. It makes sure the cells don't get too hot or too cold. These conditions help the cells continue to live and grow.

CRUELITY FREE - SAFE - HEALTHY - ENVIRONMENTALLY FRIEND

LAB-GROWN
MEAT
BEEF

LAB-MEAT-6933

NET WT. 17OZ (482g)

CHAPTER 4

CURRENT TECHNOLOGY

In 2020, Singapore became the first country to approve the sale of lab-grown meat. A company began selling chicken nuggets. The meat was grown using stem cells from a chicken feather. Then the meat was shaped, breaded, and cooked. Each nugget was crispy on the outside and juicy on the inside.

As of 2022, lab-grown meat was not yet available in most countries.

3D printing can help scientists make more complex shapes, such as steaks.

Other types of meat are harder to copy. For example, a steak has many layers of fat. This fat makes the meat juicy and tender. Getting lab-grown meat to taste similar is tricky. However, scientists in

Japan may have found a solution. They began working with 3D printers. But instead of using ink, the printers use cells. To create steak, they add one layer of cells at a time. This process can copy the webbing of fat in regular meat. But the process is very slow. Printing even a tiny piece of meat can take weeks.

SPACE MEAT

In 2019, scientists successfully grew meat in space. Stem cells were flown to the International Space Station. There, a 3D printer made small pieces of muscle. Technology like this could provide food for people living on space stations. It could also help astronauts grow meat during long missions in space.

CHAPTER 5

FUTURISTIC FOOD

As of 2022, lab-grown meat was not sold in most restaurants or stores. Its high price was one reason. In 2013, a lab-grown burger cost $325,000. By 2022, the cost had gone down to approximately $10. However, a regular burger patty was less than $2.

Scientists are exploring several ways to lower the cost of lab-grown meat.

The biggest expense is growth factor solution. This mixture helps the cells keep dividing and growing. However, the process to make it is extremely complex and expensive. It also requires animal blood **serum**.

Some researchers have tried using okara instead of growth factor solution. Okara is a pulp left over from making soy-based foods such as tofu. Like growth factor, it contains protein and hormones. But it is much less expensive. In addition, okara is plant-based. Scientists are also exploring other ways to replace serum.

To form muscle tissue, cells need a surface to attach to. So, scientists look

Okara (right) comes from soybeans (left). So, using it doesn't require harming any animals.

for low-cost **scaffolding**. One method uses blades of grass. First, scientists empty a grass blade of its own cells. Then, they inject animal cells into it. The cells receive support from the grass. They link up to form muscle tissue. Methods like this one could help lab-grown meat cost less.

People have already begun buying and getting used to plant-based meats.

Another challenge is how people think of lab-grown meat. Some people find it unnatural. They believe regular meat is healthier. However, on a basic level, lab-grown meat is identical to regular meat. It has the same animal cells. They were just grown outside an animal's body. In addition, scientists can control the ingredients of lab-grown meat. They can make it have less unhealthy fat. And they can add vitamins. As a result, lab-grown meat may actually be more nutritious.

Challenges remain. Even so, lab-grown meat has many benefits. It offers people a way to enjoy food with less harm to animals and the environment.

PLANT-BASED MEAT

Food scientists have created plant-based meat alternatives. They take protein from plants such as wheat, peas, or soybeans. The protein is heated, ground, and cooled. This process gives it a meat-like texture. Beet juice can be used to brighten the color. And coconut oil adds fat. Stores and restaurants sell a variety of plant-based meats. They include burgers, bacon, and nuggets.

FOCUS ON
LAB-GROWN MEAT

Write your answers on a separate piece of paper.

1. Write a sentence that describes the main ideas of Chapter 2.

2. Do you think lab-grown meat will ever totally replace meat from livestock? Why or why not?

3. What type of cells does lab-grown meat begin with?

   A. bone cells
   B. muscle cells
   C. stem cells

4. What might happen if more lab-grown meat used okara instead of growth factor?

   A. The price of lab-grown meat might increase.
   B. The price of lab-grown meat might decrease.
   C. The price of lab-grown meat might stay the same.

Answer key on page 32.

GLOSSARY

cell lines
Sets of cells that are the same type and grown in a lab.

climate change
A human-caused global crisis involving long-term changes in Earth's temperature and weather patterns.

ethical
Related to doing what is right.

greenhouse gas
A gas that traps heat in Earth's atmosphere, causing climate change.

hormones
Chemicals that control how certain cells grow.

protein
A substance in the body that tells a living cell what to do.

scaffolding
A structure that provides shape or support.

serum
A yellowish liquid that is part of blood.

stem cells
Cells that can develop into more-specialized cells.

tissue
A group of cells that have joined together.

TO LEARN MORE

BOOKS

Alkire, Jessie. *Farm Animal Rights*. Minneapolis: Abdo Publishing, 2018.

Kehoe, Rachel. *Improving Farming and Food Science to Fight Climate Change*. Lake Elmo, MN: Focus Readers, 2023.

McCarthy, Cecilia Pinto. *Eating Bugs as Sustainable Food*. Minneapolis: Abdo Publishing, 2020.

NOTE TO EDUCATORS

Visit **www.focusreaders.com** to find lesson plans, activities, links, and other resources related to this title.

INDEX

Answer Key: 1. Answers will vary; **2.** Answers will vary; **3.** C; **4.** B